manuel espinosa

manuel espinosa

Stephen Friedman Gallery
Sicardi Gallery

manuel espinosa: light, colour and vibration

Cristina Rossi

After the Second World War, a group of artists from the River Plate region of Argentina tried to overcome the melancholy of that ruined time by putting their creative energy and political commitment to work making something they called Concrete Art. Though polemical at first, this tendency left an indelible mark on Argentinian art history and was a spearhead for the inclusion of Latin American Constructive Art on the international map.

Manuel Espinosa was at the forefront of this movement of young artists who – rather than addressing a humanity dominated by the fears brought on by the war – preferred to create art that emphasised joy while looking ahead toward the society of the future.

These artists were opposed to any illusory form of 'representing' reality, instead 'presenting' forms that were pure invention. Their aesthetic program was based on the use of simple geometric forms – triangles, squares, circles – painted in flat colours and combined in different ways.

The origins of this concept may be traced to some of the ideas published in *Arturo: Revista de artes abstractas* in the essay 'A proposito Del marco' (A Propos of the Frame), for example. Here, Rhod Rothfuss advocated breaking with the orthogonal format that forced painting to submit to the notion of the 'Renaissance window.' Arising from this first group that formed around the abstract art journal *Arturo*, there soon emerged two more groups of artists who at the outset produced works with irregular frames or coplanar works. The first was the Asociación de Arte Concreto Invención (AACI), founded by Tomás Maldonado, Manuel Espinosa, Alfredo Hlito, Claudio Girola, Enio Iommi, Raúl Lozza and other young artists; and the second was Madí, whose members included Carmelo Arden Quin, Rhod Rothfuss, Gyula Kosice and Martín Blaszko.

During this period, Espinosa's work was based on simple forms: in some cases, irregular geometric shapes that were cut out and joined together with bars (a process that concrete artists used to create coplanar works that were attached directly to the wall), and in others, works with irregular frames whose outer edges corresponded to the geometric shapes they contained. Ten years older than most AACI members, Espinosa had already experienced an initial phase of figurative painting with a surrealistic stamp. However, he quickly integrated himself into the group and became an active participant in its avant-garde concepts.

During those years, the emergence of concrete art sparked fervent discussion with those artists who worked in the locally predominant figurative style. Such debates forced emerging artists to come up with new strategies to defend their new art form, and to that end they wrote manifestos, distributed pamphlets, published magazines and expounded their ideas in lecture halls and public talks.

Early on, Espinosa took his own stand in the polemic by responding to the survey '¿Adónde va la pintura?' (Where Is Painting Headed?), published by the magazine *Contrápunto* in August 1945. His position was that painting needed to abandon all figurative reminiscences and base itself solely on the material reality of the plane and on the work's structure.

Alongside his response to the survey, the magazine reproduced his work *Painting*, featuring an irregular frame that 'presented' irregular geometric shapes separated by black lines. On the facing page, the magazine reproduced *White Table* by the well-known artist Emilio Pettoruti. Despite its interpretation based on a synthesis of modern visual languages, it still 'represented' a still life on a white table.

As a member of the AACI, Espinosa participated in its group shows from 1946 onward, including the first show to be held at the Galería Peuser, Buenos Aires. He was one of the signers of the well-known Inventionist Manifesto, distributed on the day of the gallery's opening. On 11 September 1947, he opened a joint exhibition with Tomás Maldonado in the Argentine Society of Visual Artists exhibition space. It included a prologue by Edgar Maldonado Bayley – the poet of the group and brother of

manuel espinosa: luz, color y vibración

Cristina Rossi

Al finalizar la Segunda Guerra Mundial un grupo de artistas rioplatenses intentó barrer la melancolía de ese tiempo de despojos a partir de una propuesta de arte concreto, concebida desde el 'júbilo creador' y el compromiso político que consideraban indispensable para superar ese período de destrucción. Polémico en sus comienzos, este arte concreto grabó una huella indeleble en la historia del arte argentino y fue una punta de lanza para la inserción del arte constructivo latinoamericano en los mapas internacionales del arte moderno.

Manuel Espinosa protagonizó ese movimiento de jóvenes que –en lugar de interpretar al hombre dominado por los miedos de la guerra– prefirió crear un arte que exaltara la alegría y mirara hacia la sociedad del futuro. Estos artistas se oponían a toda forma de 'representación' ilusoria de la realidad y proponían en cambio la 'presentación' de formas de pura invención. Su programa estético partía del empleo de figuras geométricas simples –triángulos, cuadrados o círculos– pintadas con colores planos y combinadas de diferentes modos.

El origen de esta propuesta ya se encontraba en las ideas publicadas en *Arturo. Revista de artes abstractas*, donde apareció el artículo 'El marco: un problema de plástica actual'. En ese texto Rhod Rothfuss postuló la necesidad de quebrar el formato ortogonal que sujetaba a la pintura a la idea de la 'ventana renacentista'.

A partir de esa primera agrupación nucleada alrededor de *Arturo* pronto surgieron dos grupos que, en sus comienzos, realizaron obras de marco recortado y coplanares: por un lado la Asociación de Arte Concreto Invención (AACI), formada por Tomás Maldonado, Espinosa, Alfredo Hlito, Claudio Girola, Enio Iommi, Raúl Lozza y otros jóvenes artistas y, por otro lado, el grupo Madí, entre quienes se contaban Carmelo Arden Quin, Rothfuss, Gyula Kosice y Martín Blaszko.

En este período Espinosa trabajó a partir de formas simples, en algunos casos figuras geométricas irregulares recortadas y unidas con varillas –procedimiento que los artistas concretos emplearon para crear sus obras coplanares que se colocaban directamente sobre el muro– y en otros realizó obras de marco recortado, cuyos bordes se ceñían a las formas geométricas que contenían. Diez años mayor que el promedio de los integrantes de la AACI, Espinosa ya había desarrollado una primera etapa de pintura figurativa de cuño surrealizante. Sin embargo, rápidamente se integró al grupo y fue un activo participante en los planteos vanguardistas.

Eran tiempos en los que la irrupción del arte concreto había encendido fuertes discusiones con los artistas que trabajaban dentro de la figuración dominante en la escena local. Esos debates obligaron a los jóvenes a extremar las estrategias para defender su arte nuevo, razón por la cual escribieron manifiestos, repartieron panfletos, editaron revistas y predicaron sus ideas desde las aulas o en conferencias públicas.

Espinosa tempranamente enfrentó estas polémicas al responder a la encuesta ¿Adónde va la pintura? que circuló en agosto de 1945 en la revista *Contrapunto*. Frente a ese interrogante, sostuvo que la pintura debía abandonar todas las reminiscencias figurativas para apoyarse únicamente en la realidad material del plano y de la estructura de la obra.

Junto a esta respuesta se publicó su obra *Pintura*: un trabajo de marco recortado que 'presentaba' formas geométricas irregulares separadas por líneas negras. En el otro extremo de la página, la revista ubicó *Mesa Blanca* del artista ya consagrado Emilio Pettoruti que, a pesar de estar interpretada desde la síntesis de un lenguaje plástico moderno, aún 'representaba' una naturaleza muerta sobre esa mesa.

Como miembro de la AACI, desde 1946 Espinosa participó en sus muestras colectivas. Entre ellas integró la primera exposición realizada en la Galería Peuser y fue uno de los firmantes del conocido 'Manifiesto Invencionista', distribuido el día de la inauguración. El 11 septiembre de 1947 presentó una exhibición junto a Maldonado en la sala de la Sociedad Argentina de Artistas Plásticos, que contó con un prólogo de Edgar Maldonado Bayley

The magazine *Contrapunto* 1:5
(August 1945), pp.10–11

J.J. Bajarlía, 'El arte abstracto,'
Cabalgata 15 (Buenos Aires,
January 1948), p.5

Untitled, 1958, oil on canvas,
75 × 40 cm (29½ × 16 in)
Collection of Ernesto & Cecilia Poma

Untitled, 1961, oil on canvas,
80 × 35 cm (31½ × 14 in)

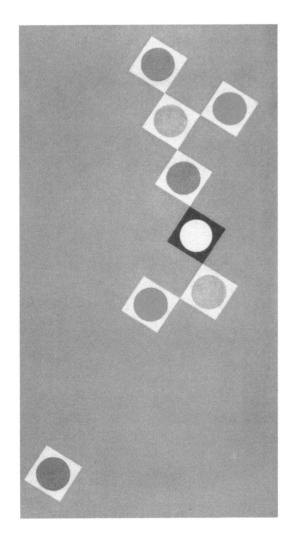

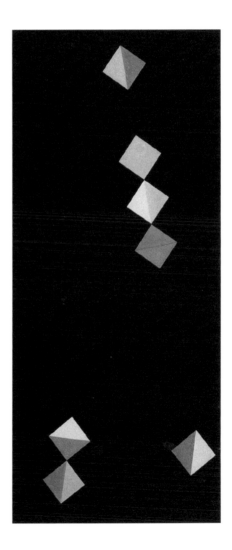

Tomás – which drew attention to the subtle tonal relationships already present in Espinosa's work.

Around 1948, the postwar reconstruction process in Europe made it possible to travel to that continent again. The first one to visit the major European capitals was Tomás Maldonado, followed by Arden Quin, Juan Melé and Gregorio Vardanega. When Espinosa was planning his first trip to Europe in 1951, he plotted a route based on the advice of his friend Maldonado. His itinerary took him to Italy, Switzerland, Paris, Belgium and Holland, and along the way he met Piero Dorazio, Bruno Munari, Max Huber, Max Bill, Richard P. Lohse, Verena Loewensberg and Georges Vantongerloo, among others. He was the first among his peers to go to Amsterdam, where he made the acquaintance of the De Stijl artist Friedrich Vordemberge Gildewart.

Espinosa's poetics continued along the path of renovation, and upon returning from his European trip, he initiated a period of intense exploration, painting mainly with tempera. In dialogue with Loewensberg, Gildewart, Vantongerloo and Bill, he reinterpreted some of the styles that appeared frequently in these artists' concrete works. His works on paper from this period – which he showed at Galería Van Riel in Buenos Aires in 1959 – present a re-thinking of the figure-ground relationship and a return to more traditional formats, having abandoned his irregular frames.

While the 1940s represented a time of radical departures in concrete art among the avant-garde artists of the River Plate region, during the 1950s many of these same artists began forming new groups to consolidate and develop abstract languages in all the variants being developed in Argentina. Some artists' initiatives – such as the 'Exhibition of Non-Figurative Art' held in 1960 in Raúl Lozza's studio under the auspices of the Museum of Modern Art – gathered all the abstract tendencies together, while others such as 'Form and Space: First International Exhibition' promoted interchange among the region's different productions. Espinosa participated in both shows, and at the latter one in 1962, he signed the Manifesto of Constructive Painters from Argentina, Chile and Uruguay, which rejected gestural and informalist abstract expressions.

This show, held in Santiago de Chile, presented Espinosa's paintings from the series he did in tempera during the late 1950s, with a visual vocabulary based on squares, triangles and circles. In these works, the quadrangular forms were by turns very lightly delineated, dotted or accentuated, painted in flat colours or formed by the juxtaposition of two triangles. The squares sometimes contained circles painted in solid colours or sfumato, and in terms of the organisation of the visual field, there was already a marked tendency toward the generation of groupings that added tension to the composition.

In the early 1960s, Espinosa returned to Europe where he travelled through Spain and then settled in Italy. For a time, he participated in the Roman art scene, making contact with young Italian artists who were experimenting with Op Art. He also produced works linked to textile design and showed his earliest works in the Op Art tendency.

On returning to Buenos Aires, he put both lines of work into practice. He entered his designs for textiles for clothing and interior decoration into a contest. He played freely with colour and texture in creating the fabric patterns, even basing them on ripped paper or collage. He also produced a series of optical works on paper, many of them done with a ruling pen and coloured inks, though he sometimes limited himself to a black and white palette. His white paintings on white backgrounds rely on the subtlety of minimal contrast, while the black-on-white designs present strong contrasts and vibratory effects.

During this period he also intensified his work based on the circle as a visual element, applying the concepts of serialisation and vibration advanced by Op Art. Circular forms multiplied and were arranged in series until they occupied the entire surface of the canvas. Over the series of shifting circles he used a subtly graduated colour scale that produced a sense of movement while also generating oscillations.

–el poeta del grupo y hermano de Tomás– quien destacó las sutiles relaciones tonales que ya presentaba la obra de Espinosa.

Hacia 1948, el proceso de reconstrucción europea había reabierto la posibilidad de embarcarse desde América hacia esos rumbos. El primero en visitar las principales capitales europeas fue Maldonado quien, luego, fue seguido por Arden Quin, Juan Melé y Gregorio Vardanega. En 1951 –cuando proyectó su primer viaje a Europa– Espinosa trazó el itinerario siguiendo los consejos de su amigo Tomás. Su recorrido incluyó la visita a Italia, Suiza, París, Bélgica y Holanda, donde se acercó a Piero Dorazio, Bruno Munari, Max Huber, Max Bill, Richard P. Lohse, Verena Loewensberg y Georges Vantongerloo, entre otros, y fue el primero en llegar a Amsterdam para relacionarse con Vordemberge Gildewart.

La poética de Espinosa no abandonó el camino de la renovación y, al regresar de este viaje, comenzó una etapa de profundización de sus indagaciones en la que pintó, principalmente, con témpera. En diálogo con Loewensberg, Vordemberge Gildewart, Vantongerloo o Bill, reinterpretó algunos estilemas frecuentes en las obras concretas de estos artistas. Los trabajos sobre papel de este período –que exhibió en la Galería Van Riel en 1959– retomaron la relación figura-fondo y volvieron a los formatos tradicionales, alejados ya de las propuestas de marco recortado.

Si para los vanguardistas rioplatenses los años 40 habían sido los tiempos de las rupturas radicales del arte concreto, durante los 50 muchos de ellos tendieron a reagruparse para consolidar y expandir el lenguaje abstracto en todas las variantes desarrolladas en la Argentina. Algunas iniciativas de los artistas, como la *Exposición de Arte no Figurativo* que se realizó 1960 en el taller de Raúl Lozza con el auspicio del Museo de Arte Moderno de Buenos Aires, reunían a todas las tendencias de la abstracción, mientras que otras como la *1ª Muestra Internacional Forma y Espacio* propiciaban el intercambio entre las producciones de la región. Espinosa participó de ambas y en esta última suscribió el 'Manifiesto de los pintores constructivos de Argentina, Chile y Uruguay' que, en 1962, rechazaba a las expresiones de la abstracción gestual e informalista.

En esta muestra, organizada en Santiago de Chile, presentó pinturas que correspondían a las series realizadas en témpera a finales de los 50, dentro de un vocabulario plástico que partía del cuadrado, el triángulo y el círculo. En estas obras, los motivos cuadrangulares aparecen apenas delineados, punteados o remarcados, pintados con colores planos o formados por la yuxtaposición de dos triángulos. En ocasiones los cuadrados incluyen formas circulares pintadas con colores plenos o difuminados. En la organización del campo visual, ya se percibe la tendencia a generar agrupamientos que tensionan la composición.

En los primeros años de la década del 60 Espinosa volvió a viajar a Europa, recorrió España y se estableció en Italia. Durante un tiempo se insertó en el medio cultural romano, donde tomó contacto con los jóvenes italianos que incursionaban en el *op-art*, realizó trabajos vinculados con el diseño textil y exhibió las primeras obras que pintó dentro de la variante óptica.

Al regresar a Buenos Aires puso en práctica ambas líneas de trabajo. Por un lado presentó en un concurso sus diseños para telas de indumentaria y de uso hogareño, con motivos en los que jugó libremente con el color y la textura e, incluso, compuso desgarrando el papel o sumando el *collage*. Por otro lado desarrolló una serie de trabajos ópticos sobre papel, muchos de ellos realizados con tiralíneas y tintas de color, en otros casos, recurrió sólo al registro del blanco y negro. Las pinturas blancas sobre fondo blanco apelan a la sutileza del contraste mínimo, mientras que los diseños en negro sobre fondos blancos provocan fuertes contrastes y efectos vibratorios.

En esta época también profundizó su trabajo sobre el círculo como tema plástico, al que aplicó los conceptos de serialización y vibración que incluían los programas del *op-art*. Las formas circulares se fueron multiplicando y –dispuestas en serie– ocuparon toda la superficie de la tela. Sobre la serie de círculos

Untitled, 1975, lithographic ink on
paper, 50 × 65.5 cm (20 × 26 in)

C-CB-CE, *c.*1960, ink on paper,
37 × 55 cm (14½ × 21½ in)
Private Collection, New York

Axchewzi, 1972, acrylic on canvas,
100 × 100 cm (39½ × 39½ in)
Private Collection, Houston

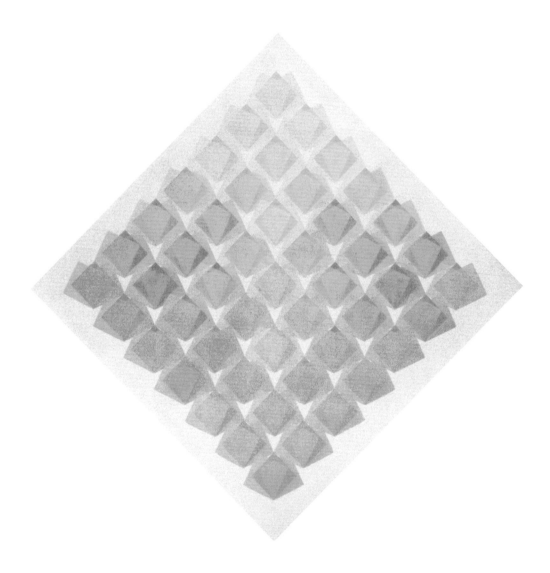

In the late 1970s he exhibited these paintings in the avant-garde spaces of the Torcuato Di Tella Institute and at the National Museum of Fine Arts, where he presented an installation entitled '18 Variations on a Theme: Diminuendo and Crescendo in Blue', deploying the colour scale over the walls and floor.

Over time, Espinosa began alternating between painting on canvas and drawing on paper. The smaller format gave him more freedom and space for experimentation. One such series explored centrifugal movement based on criss-crossing lines. In some cases, the forces are stabilised within an orthogonal organisation, while in others, oblique lines generate dynamic tension that radiates from the centre to the outer edge of these compositions.

Based on the repetition of a serialised module, he later experimented with the use of graphite and tempera. His interest lay not only in the regularity of the series, but also in the modulation of the grid, because by slightly transgressing the sequence's rhythm, he was able to produce alterations in the weave that produced optical illusions.

In this line of experimentation, Espinosa worked with lithographic inks. Often used in industrial printing, these quick-drying inks lent his works a smooth finish. During the 1970s, he produced linear series on a variety of supports with different dimensions, applying the medium with an ink roller to achieve different degrees of density and transparency.

Both his optical works – which challenge the spectator's gaze with paradoxical situations – and his linear series were exhibited in Argentina and internationally. The former were primarily shown at the Buenos Aires gallery Arte Nuevo and in the Nigerian city of Lagos, while the latter were shown in a 1974 exhibition in Venezuela.

In the early 1970s, Espinosa began to show a preference for the square as a motif and acrylic paints as a medium, allowing him to handle transparencies with greater ease and multiplying the range of shadows and shades cast by each module in the series. The closeness or distance of a single form brought the space-time dimension into play through the forms' superimposition and arrangement into ordered lines. The use of illuminated areas, tensions and colour accents allowed him to instil each work with a unique character, thus obliging the gaze to enter the painting guided by one or several modules until it became submerged in the internal dynamic governing the composition as a whole.

Rhythm and serialisation – fundamental components of Espinosa's poetics – predominated in the overlapping domains of painting, music and poetry that so fascinated the artist. Adhering to that dynamic, many of his works' titles made reference to the creative universe of the artists he admired, such as James Joyce, Erik Satie and Duke Ellington. In other cases he simply relied on modes of organisation – such as repetition – that abounded in the musical works and poems which inspired his paintings. For example, he invented nearly unpronounceable words (axchewzl or apanasss) for some of his works' titles; rather than remitting to a specific meaning, they suggest the musicality of a series of rhythms or a colour scheme, as in Arthur Rimbaud's sonnet alluding to the material aspect of writing through the visual sensation of colour: 'A noir, E blanc, I rouge, U vert, O bleu: voyelles' (A black, E white, I red, U green, O blue: vowels).

In short, Manuel Espinosa was a master of the use of shades and nuances, a 'seeker of harmonies' who chose tones and semitones, as Marta Traba once wrote. Though he preferred murmured tones to more strident ones, his control of the subtleties of light and colour cause our emotions to vibrate at the highest of notes.

Translated by Michelle Suderman

que se van desplazando, empleó una escala cromática sutilmente graduada que provoca la percepción de un movimiento en profundidad que a la vez, genera oscilaciones.

Hacia finales de los años sesenta exhibió estas pinturas tanto en las salas del vanguardista Instituto Torcuato Di Tella como en el Museo Nacional de Bellas Artes, donde presentó una instalación que desplegaba la escala cromática en las paredes y el piso, titulada '18 variaciones sobre un tema: diminuendo and crescendo in blue'.

A través del tiempo Espinosa fue alternando la pintura sobre tela y el dibujo. Los formatos más reducidos le proporcionaron un alto grado de libertad y espacio para la experimentación. Una serie de estos trabajos exploró el movimiento centrífugo a partir de entrecruzamientos lineales. En algunos, las fuerzas se estabilizan dentro de una organización ortogonal, mientras que en otros la línea oblicua genera una tensión dinámica que se dirige desde el centro hasta los límites de estas composiciones.

Sobre la base de la repetición de un módulo serializado, más tarde experimentó con el grafito y la témpera. Su interés no sólo radicaba en la regularidad de la serie, sino también en la modulación de la grilla, porque al transgredir levemente el ritmo de la secuencia lograba producir modificaciones en la trama que generaban ilusiones ópticas.

Dentro de esta línea de trabajo empleó tintas litográficas que, por su uso en la impresión industrial, le permitían lograr un acabado parejo y secado rápido. En los años 70 produjo series lineales en las que fue variando el tipo y las medidas del soporte sobre los que aplicaba la materia con rodillo para lograr diferentes calidades por densidad y transparencia.

Tanto las propuestas ópticas –que ponían a la mirada del espectador frente a situaciones paradojales– como estas series lineales fueron exhibidas en salas argentinas e internacionales. Las primeras se expusieron en la galería porteña Arte Nuevo y en la ciudad nigeriana de Lagos, mientras que las segundas integraron la exposición *Manuel Espinosa* presentada en 1974 en el Centro Venezolano-Argentino de Cooperación Cultural y Científico-Tecnológica de Caracas.

A principios de los 70 comenzó a tomar protagonismo el cuadrado y Espinosa incorporó la pintura acrílica, material que le facilitó el manejo de las transparencias y la multiplicación de la gama de sombras que podía arrojar cada módulo de la serie. El acercamiento o alejamiento de una misma forma ponía en juego la dimensión espacio-temporal a través del despliegue y la superposición. El manejo de las zonas iluminadas, las tensiones y los acentos de color le permitían marcar el carácter de cada obra. Así lograba, que la mirada del espectador ingresara guiada por uno o varios módulos y que se fuera sumergiendo en la dinámica interna que regía toda esa composición.

El ritmo y la serialización –componentes fundamentales de la poética de Espinosa– reinaban en el territorio común de la pintura, la música y la poesía que lo seducían. Siguiendo esa dinámica, tituló muchas obras haciendo referencia al universo creativo de los artistas que admiraba, como James Joyce, Erik Satie o Duke Ellington. En otros casos sólo recurrió a las modalidades de organización, como la repetición que regía en las obras musicales o en los poemas con los que se correspondía su pintura. Para nombrar algunas obras compuso palabras casi impronunciables (axchewzl o apanasss) que, antes que remitir a un significado, sugieren la musicalidad de una serie de compases o un colorido, como en el soneto de Arthur Rimbaud que alude a la materia de su escritura según la sensación visual del color: 'A noir, E blanc, I rouge, U vert, O bleu: voyelles'.

En suma, Manuel Espinosa ha sido un maestro en el manejo de los matices, un 'perseguidor de armonías' que – como alguna vez escribió Marta Traba – escogía cuidadosamente los tonos y semitonos. Dueño de una personalidad que prefería el murmullo antes que las estridencias, en su pintura supo dominar las sutilezas del color y de la luz para hacer vibrar las notas más altas de nuestras emociones.

plates

16   *Orex*, 1968, oil on canvas, 125 × 125 cm (49 × 49 in)

17

Ubeq, 1968, oil on canvas, 125 × 125 cm (49 × 49 in)

Untitled, *c.*1970, oil on canvas, 125 × 125 cm (49 × 49 in)

22   *Untitled*, *c.* 1970, oil on canvas, 125 × 125 cm (49 × 49 in)

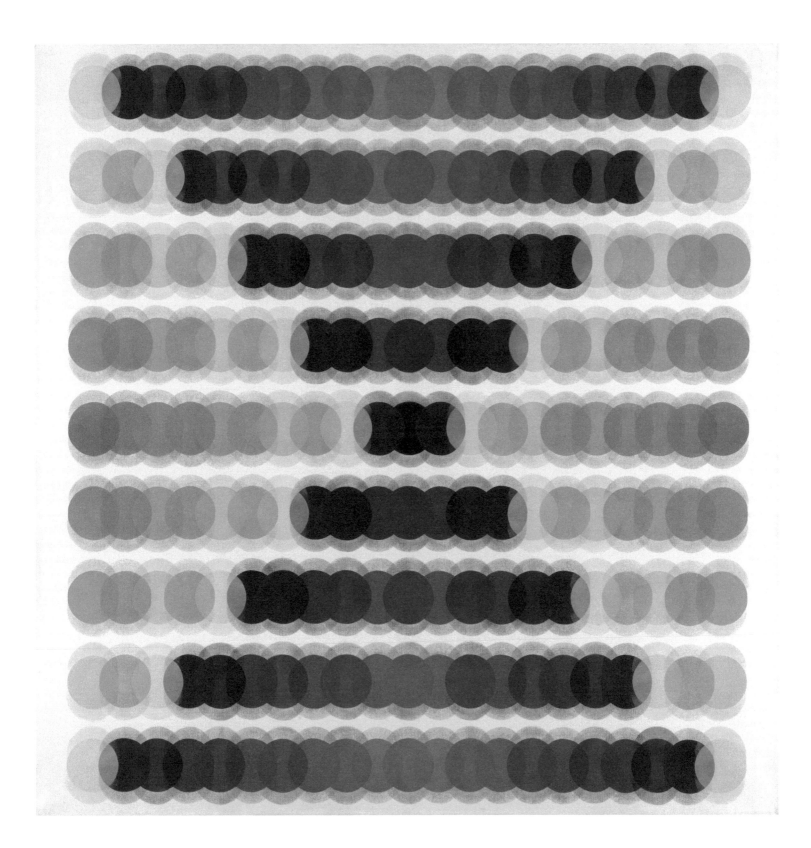

Untitled, *c*.1970, oil on canvas, 150 × 100 cm (59 × 39½ in)

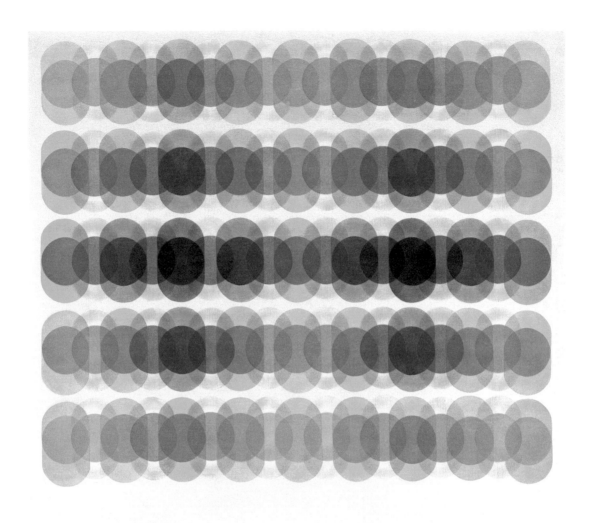

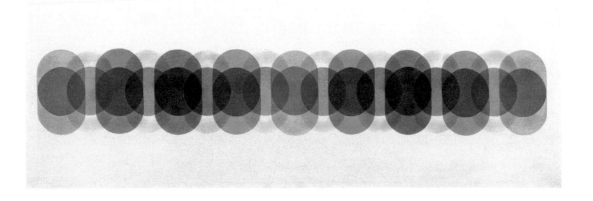

Rosebud, 1970, oil on canvas, 150 × 150 cm (59 × 59 in)

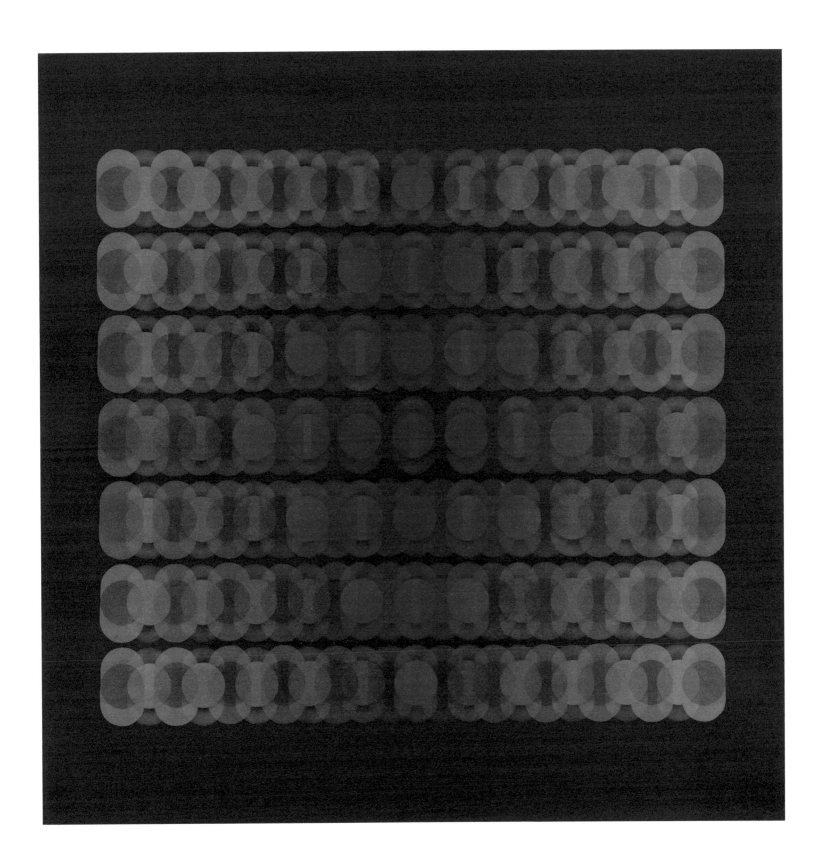

Untitled, *c.*1960, tempera on paper, 28 × 38 cm (11 × 15 in)

Untitled, c.1960, tempera on paper, 28 × 38 cm (11 × 15 in)

Untitled, c.1970, lithographic ink on paper, 32.5 × 25 cm (13 × 10 in)

32   *Untitled*, *c.*1970, lithographic ink on paper, 32.5 × 25 cm (13 × 10 in)

Untitled, *c.*1970, lithographic ink on paper, 32.5 × 25 cm (13 × 10 in)

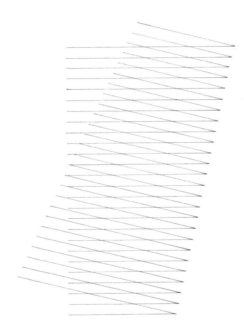

Untitled, *c.*1970, ink on paper, 48.5 × 65 cm (19 × 25½ in)

Untitled, *c.*1970, ink on paper, 48.5 × 65 cm (19 × 25½ in)

Untitled, *c.*1970, ink on paper, 48.5 × 65 cm (19 × 25½ in)

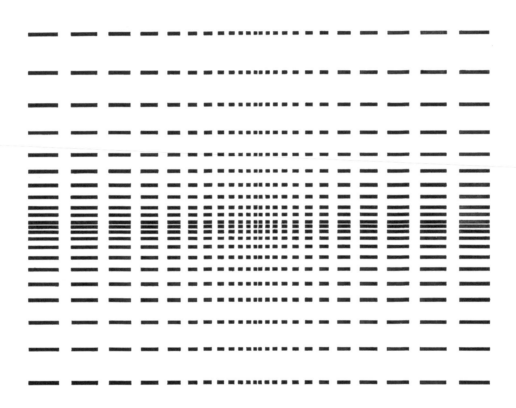

Untitled, *c.*1970, ink on paper, 48.5 × 65 cm (19 × 25½ in)

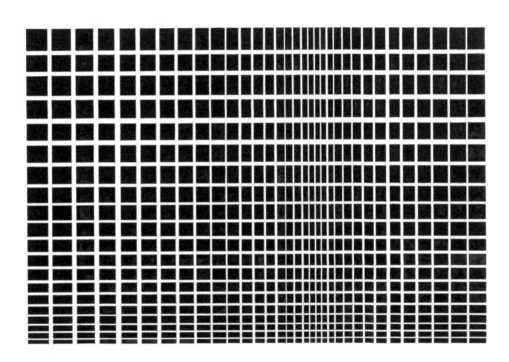

Untitled, *c.*1970, ink on paper, 48.5 × 65 cm (19 × 25½ in)

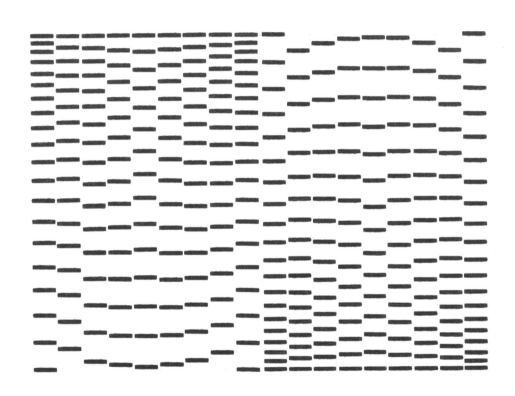

Untitled, 1975, graphite on paper, 48.5 × 65.5 cm (19 × 26 in)

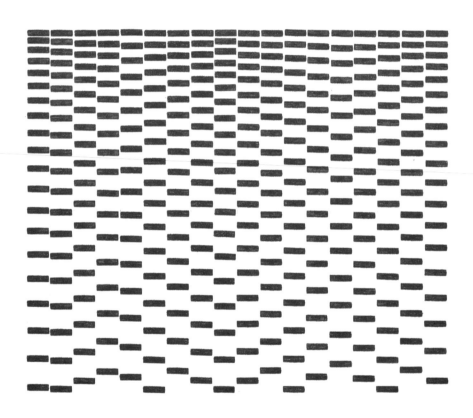

Untitled, 1975, graphite on paper, 48.5 × 65.5 cm (19 × 26 in)

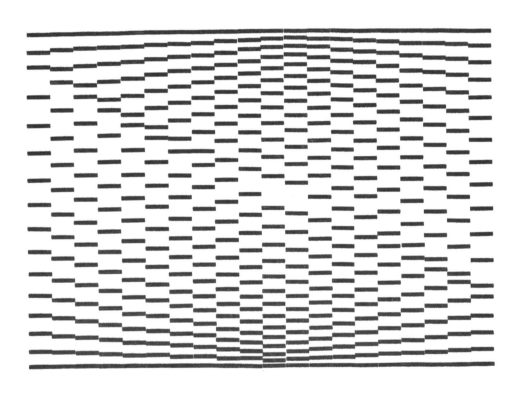

Untitled, 1975, graphite on paper, 48.5 × 65.5 cm (19 × 26 in)

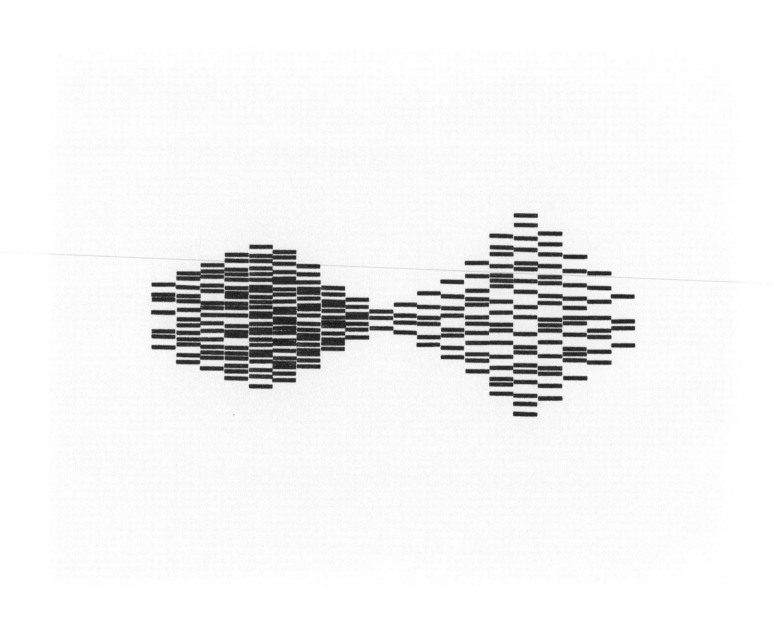

Untitled, 1975, graphite on paper, 48.5 × 64 cm (19 × 25 in)

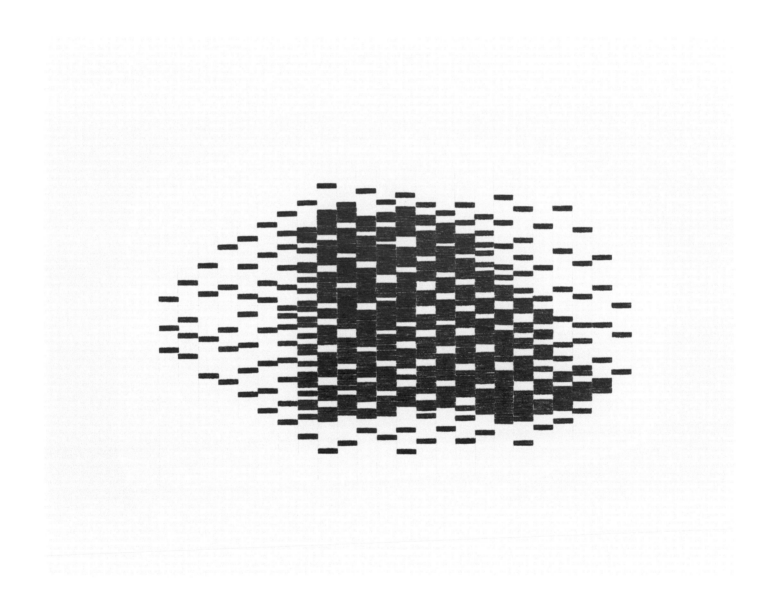

Untitled, 1975, graphite on paper, 48.5 × 64 cm (19 × 25 in)

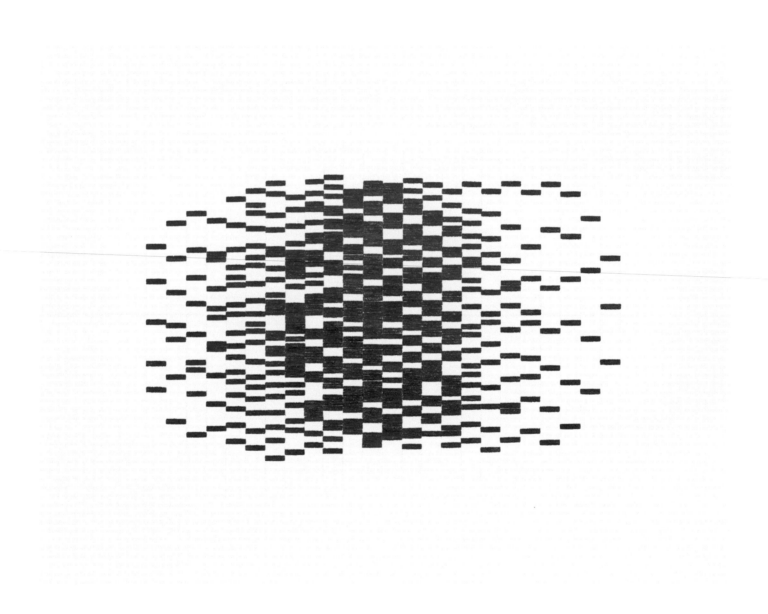

Untitled, 1975, graphite on paper, 48.5 × 64 cm (19 × 25 in)

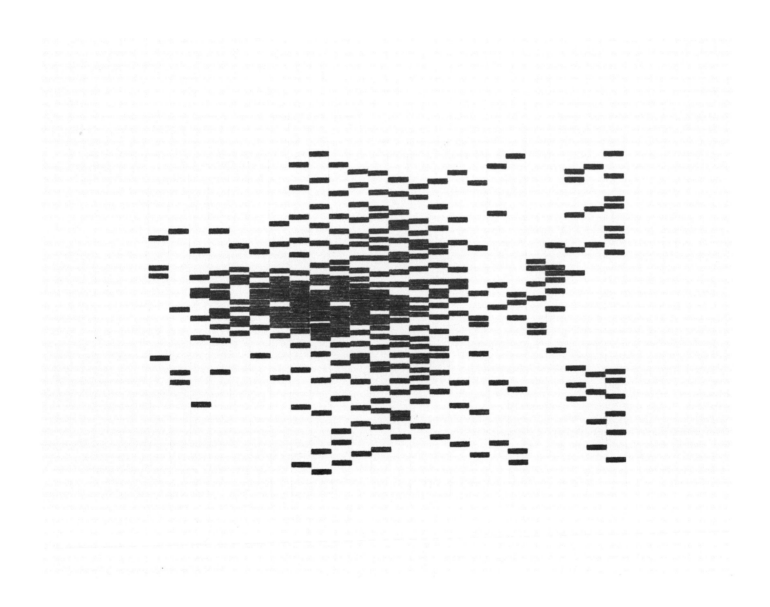

Untitled, 1975, graphite on paper, 48.5 × 64 cm (19 × 25 in)

Untitled, 1975, lithographic ink on paper, 50 × 65.5 cm (20 × 26 in)

Untitled, 1981, tempera on paper, 70 × 50 cm (27½ × 19½ in)

Untitled, 1981, tempera on paper, 70 × 50 cm (27½ × 19½ in)

Untitled, 1981, ink on paper, 40 × 50 cm (16 × 19½ in)

Untitled, 1981, ink on paper, 40 × 50 cm (16 × 19½ in)

Untitled, 1981, ink on paper, 40 × 50 cm (16 × 19½ in)

Untitled, 1981, ink on paper, 40 × 50 cm (16 × 19½ in)

Untitled, 1983, ink on paper, 65 × 40.5 cm (25½ × 16 in)

Untitled, 1983, ink on paper, 65 × 40.5 cm (25½ × 16 in)

catalogue list (dimensions are paper size)

Orex, 1968
oil on canvas
125 × 125 cm (49 × 49 in)
p.17

Ubeq, 1968
oil on canvas
125 × 125 cm (49 × 49 in)
p.19

Untitled, c.1970
oil on canvas
125 × 125 cm (49 × 49 in)
p.21

Untitled, c.1970
oil on canvas
125 × 125 cm (49 × 49 in)
p.23

Untitled, c.1970
oil on canvas
150 × 100 cm (59 × 39½ in)
p.25

Rosebud, 1970
oil on canvas
150 × 150 cm (59 × 59 in)
p.27

Untitled, c.1960
tempera on paper
28 × 38 cm (11 × 15 in)
p.28

Untitled, c.1960
tempera on paper
28 × 38 cm (11 × 15 in)
p.29

Untitled, c.1970
lithographic ink on paper
32.5 × 25 cm (13 × 10 in)
p.31

Untitled, c.1970
lithographic ink on paper
32.5 × 25 cm (13 × 10 in)
p.32

Untitled, c.1970
lithographic ink on paper
32.5 × 25 cm (13 × 10 in)
p.33

Untitled, c.1970
ink on paper
48.5 × 65 cm (19 × 25½ in)
p.35

Untitled, c.1970
ink on paper
48.5 × 65 cm (19 × 25½ in)
p.36

Untitled, c.1970
ink on paper
48.5 × 65 cm (19 × 25½ in)
p.37

Untitled, c.1970
ink on paper
48.5 × 65 cm (19 × 25½ in)
p.38

Untitled, c.1970
ink on paper
48.5 × 65 cm (19 × 25½ in)
p.39

Untitled, 1975
graphite on paper
48.5 × 65.5 cm (19 × 26 in)
p.41

Untitled, 1975
graphite on paper
48.5 × 65.5 cm (19 × 26 in)
p.42

Untitled, 1975
graphite on paper
48.5 × 65.5 cm (19 × 26 in)
p.43

Untitled, 1975
graphite on paper
48.5 × 64 cm (19 × 25 in)
p.44

Untitled, 1975
graphite on paper
48.5 × 64 cm (19 × 25 in)
p.45

Untitled, 1975
graphite on paper
48.5 × 64 cm (19 × 25 in)
p.46

Untitled, 1975
graphite on paper
48.5 × 64 cm (19 × 25 in)
p.47

Untitled, 1975
lithographic ink on paper
50 × 65.5 cm (20 × 26 in)
p.48

Untitled, 1975
lithographic ink on paper
50 × 65.5 cm (20 × 26 in)
p.49

Untitled, 1981
tempera on paper
70 × 50 cm (27½ × 19½ in)
p.50

Untitled, 1981
tempera on paper
70 × 50 cm (27½ × 19½ in)
p.51

Untitled, 1981
ink on paper
40 × 50 cm (16 × 19½ in)
p.52

Untitled, 1981
ink on paper
40 × 50 cm (16 × 19½ in)
p.53

Untitled, 1981
ink on paper
40 × 50 cm (16 × 19½ in)
p.54

Untitled, 1981
ink on paper
40 × 50 cm (16 × 19½ in)
p.55

Untitled, 1983
ink on paper
65 × 40.5 cm (25½ × 16 in)
p.57

Untitled, 1983
ink on paper
65 × 40.5 cm (25½ × 16 in)
p.58

Untitled, 1983
ink on paper
65 × 40.5 cm (25½ × 16 in)
p.59

Manuel Espinosa at home

Manuel Espinosa

Born: 1912 in Buenos Aires, Argentina
Died: 2006 in Buenos Aires, Argentina

Solo Exhibitions (selected)

2014
Manuel Espinosa, Stephen Friedman Gallery, London, England

2013
Manuel Espinosa: Geometría en Movimiento, Museo de Arte Contemporáneo de Buenos Aires, Buenos Aires, Argentina
Manuel Espinosa: Paintings and Works on Paper, 1960s and 1970s, Sicardi Gallery, Houston, Texas, USA

2010
Manuel Espinosa: Drawings and Paintings, 1950s – 1970s, Sicardi Gallery, Houston, Texas, USA

2009
Espinosa, Museo Nacional de Bellas Artes, Neuquén, Argentina

2003
Manuel Espinosa. Anthology on Paper, Museo de Arte Moderno, Buenos Aires, Argentina

2001
Manuel Espinosa. Rosario Prize 2001, Museo Municipal de Bellas Artes, Rosario, Santa Fe, Argentina

1981
Manuel Espinosa, Galería del Retiro, Buenos Aires, Argentina

1980
Manuel Espinosa, National Arts Center, Ottawa, Canada; travelled to Robson Square Media Centre, Vancouver, Canada

1979
Manuel Espinosa, Galería del Retiro, Buenos Aires, Argentina
Manuel Espinosa, Argentine Embassy, Montevideo, Uruguay

1977
Manuel Espinosa, The National Gallery of Art, Lagos, Nigeria
Manuel Espinosa, Acrylic Paintings, Galería Vermeer, Buenos Aires, Argentina

1975
Manuel Espinosa, Centro de Artes y Letras, Liga de Fomento, Punta del Este, Uruguay

1974
Manuel Espinosa, Paintings, Centro Venezolano-Argentino de Cooperación Cultural y Científico-Tecnológica, Caracas, Venezuela
Manuel Espinosa, Galería Carmen Waugh, Buenos Aires, Argentina
Manuel Espinosa, Galería Contemporanea, Montevideo, Uruguay

1972
Manuel Espinosa, Galería Carmen Waugh, Buenos Aires, Argentina
Oils by Manuel Espinosa, Galería Quinta Dimensión, Buenos Aires, Argentina

1971
Manuel Espinosa, Galería del Plata, Mar de Plata, Buenos Aires, Argentina
Manuel Espinosa, Paintings, Galería Austral, La Plata, Buenos Aires, Argentina

1970
Manuel Espinosa, Pyopen or 20 variations of the same theme, Galería Arte Nuevo, Buenos Aires, Argentina

1969
Manuel Espinosa, Galería Arte Nuevo, Buenos Aires, Argentina
Manuel Espinosa, Paintings, Galería El Taller, Buenos Aires, Argentina

1968
Manuel Espinosa, Paintings, Galería El Taller, Buenos Aires, Argentina
Manuel Espinosa, Galería Arte Nuevo, Buenos Aires, Argentina

1959
Espinosa, Galería Van Riel, Buenos Aires, Argentina

1940
Manuel O. Espinosa, Teatro del Pueblo, Buenos Aires, Argentina

Group Exhibitions (selected)

2012
Real/Virtual, Arte cinético argentino de los años sesenta, Museo Nacional de Bellas Artes, Buenos Aires, Argentina
A Global exchange. Geometric abstraction since 1950, Museo de Arte Contemporáneo de Buenos Aires, Argentina

2006
Artist Collections, Fundación Proa, Buenos Aires, Argentina

2004–2005
Utopia of Form. Argentine Concrete Art, Alejandra von Hartz Fine Arts, Miami, Florida, USA

2004
Utopia of Form, Arte Concreto – Invención, Galería del Infinito, Buenos Aires, Argentina

2003
Geo-metries, Latin American Geometric Abstraction in the Cisneros Collection, Malba – Fundación Costantini, Museo de Arte Latinoamericano de Buenos Aires, Argentina

2002–2003
Argentine Abstract Art, Galleria d'Arte Moderna e Contemporanea di Bergamo, Bergamo, Italy; travelled to Fundación Proa, Buenos Aires, Argentina

2002
Argentine Art of the XX Century, Cultural Exchange, Instituto Cultural Peruano Norteamericano, Lima, Peru; travelled to Museo Provincial de Bellas Artes, Santa Fe, Argentina
Surface and Subtext: Latin American Geometric Abstraction, The Jack Blanton Museum of Art, Austin, Texas, USA

2001
Abstract Art from Rio de la Plata, Buenos Aires and Montevideo 1933–1953, The Americas Society, New York, USA

1997
Acquired Works, Palais de Glace, Buenos Aires, Argentina

1996
First Show of Paintings by the Critics, Salas Nacionales de la Cultura, Buenos Aires, Argentina

1995
Tribute to Alfredo Hlito by His Friends, Galería de Arte Julia Lublin, Buenos Aires, Argentina
50 Years of the Asociación Arte Concreto-Invención, Instituto Cultural Iberoamericano, Buenos Aires, Argentina

1994
Art from Argentina 1920/1994, Museum of Modern Art, Oxford, UK

1993
Juan Melé. Paris Period 1990/93, Centoira Galería de Arte, Buenos Aires, Argentina

1992
From Constructivism to Sensible Geometry, Harrods, Buenos Aires, Argentina

1990
The Manifesto of Realism. Moscow 1920 – Tribute by the Museo de Arte Contemporáneo, Buenos Aires 1920, Galería Vermeer, Buenos Aires, Argentina

1989
When Geometry…2. Tribute to Piet Mondrian, Museo de Arte Moderno, Buenos Aires, Argentina

1988–1989
Seven Argentine Masters, Vatus Foundation, Schaumburg, Federal Republic of Germany; travelled to Mittelrhein Museum, Coblenza, Federal Republic of Germany; Museum Moderner Kunst, Vienna, Austria; Kimberley Gallery, Washington D.C., United States; and Museo de Arte Moderno, Buenos Aires, Argentina

1987–1988
Argentine Art from the Independence to Today. 1810–1987, Instituto Italo-Latinoamericano, Rome, Italy; travelled to Instituto Italo-Latinoamericano, Genoa, Italy

1986
Argentine Plastic Arts. Selection of Works from the Citibank Collection, Museo Eduardo Sívori, Buenos Aires, Argentina
Ignacio Pirovano, an Argentine Collector, Museo de Arte Moderno, Buenos Aires, Argentina

1985
Abstraction in the XX Century, Museo de Arte Moderno, Buenos Aires, Argentina

1984
The Toy, Museo Municipal de Arte Juan Carlos Castagnino, Mar del Plata, Buenos Aires, Argentina
Artists on Paper, Centro Cultural de la Ciudad de Buenos Aires, Buenos Aires, Argentina
Criticism Conferences. From Geometry. Galería Wildestein, Buenos Aires, Argentina

1983
Geometries. Criticism Conferences 83, Asociación Internacional de Críticos de Arte, Galería Rubbers, Buenos Aires, Argentina
Tribute to Democracy by the Visual Arts. Testimony of the Vanguards, Argentina de Críticos de Arte, Museo Eduardo Sívori, Buenos Aires, Argentina

1981
Geometry 81, Museo Provincial de La Plata, La Plata, Buenos Aires, Argentina
Criticism Conferences 81, Asociación Internacional de Críticos de Arte, Galería Vermeer, Buenos Aires, Argentina

1980
Contemporary Argentine Art. The 13th International Art Exhibition. Tokyo Biennale '80, Metropolitan Museum, Tokyo, Japan; travelled to Municipal Museum of Art, Kyoto, Japan
The Space Appears so Vast to Us, Alberto Elía Galería de Arte, Buenos Aires, Argentina
Vanguards of the 1940s. Arte Concreto-Invención, Arte Madí, Perceptismo, Museo Eduardo Sívori, Buenos Aires, Argentina

1979
Tribute to Geometry, Galería Praxis, Buenos Aires, Argentina

1978
The Argentinean Exposition, The Armas Gallery, Miami, Florida, USA

1977–1979
Recent Latin American Drawings (1969/76). Lines of Vision, Center for Inter-American Relations, New York; travelled to Florida International University, Miami, Florida; The

Arkansas Arts Center, Little Rock, Arkansas; College of Fine Arts, Austin, Texas; University of Texas, Texas; Oklahoma Art Center, Oklahoma, USA; Metropolitan Museum of Manila, Manila, Philippines; Art Gallery of Hamilton, Hamilton, Ontario, Canada; Indianapolis Museum of Art, Indianapolis; Inter-American Development Bank Gallery, Washington; Vassar College Art Gallery, New York; Anchorage Historical & Fine Arts Museum, Alaska; and Munson-Williams-Proctor Institute, Utica, New York, USA

1977–1978
Current State of Young Argentine Painting, Museo de Arte Brasileira da Fundação Armando Alvares Penteado, San Pablo, Brazil

1977
Current Art of Latin America, Centro Cultural de la Villa de Madrid, Madrid, Spain
Reopening Ceremony, Galería Art, Buenos Aires, Argentina

1976
Tribute to the Argentine Vanguard of the 1940s, Galería Arte Nuevo, Buenos Aires, Argentina
From Figuration to Abstraction, Dirección de Turismo, San Miguel de Tucumán, Tucumán, Argentina
Current Argentine Painting. Two Trends: Geometry – Surrealism, Museo Nacional de Bellas Artes, Buenos Aires, Argentina

1974
Current Trends in Argentine Art, Centre Artistique de Recontres Internacionales, Ville Arson, Nice, France
Current Trends in Argentine Art, Museo Provincial de Bellas Artes, La Plata, Buenos Aires, Argentina
Manuel Espinosa and Jorge Gamarra, Galería Art, Buenos Aires, Argentina
Box Objects, Galería Arte Nuevo, Buenos Aires, Argentina
Geometric Artists Christmas Eve 74, Galería Nueva Visión, Mar del Plata, Buenos Aires, Argentina
Christmas 1974, Galería Art, Buenos Aires, Argentina

Contemporary Argentine Art. Museo de Arte Moderno de Ciudad de México, Mexico
Geometric Painting, Colegio de Escribanos, Azul, Buenos Aires, Argentina
14 Argentine Painters, Caja Nacional de Ahorro y Seguro, Buenos Aires, Argentina

1973
Projection and Dynamism. Six Argentine Painters, Musée d'Art Moderne de la Ville de Paris, Paris, France
Presence of the Museo Provincial de Bellas Artes in the City of Buenos Aires, Galería de Arte YPF, Buenos Aires, Argentina
Second Show of What We Do and What Others Do That We Like, 1249 Estudio, Buenos Aires, Argentina
Magical Abstraction 1973, Galería Art, Buenos Aires, Argentina

1972
State of Argentine Plastic Arts, Galería Quinta Dimensión, Buenos Aires, Argentina
Pablo's Identikit. Tribute to Picasso, Centro Cultural General San Martín, Buenos Aires, Argentina
Exhibition No. 11, Museo Municipal de Artes Visuales, Santa Fe, New Mexico, USA
First Countershow '72, Sociedad Central de Arquitectos, Buenos Aires, Argentina
Art and Industry, Julio Sabra and Sons, Sudamtex S. A., Montevideo, Uruguay
First Show of Works Donated to the Museo de la Solidaridad, Instituto de Arte Latinoamericano, Universidad de Chile, Santiago, Chile
Argentine Creators of Current Art. Selection 1972, Galería Rubbers, Buenos Aires, Argentina
1972: The Hundredth Anniversary of the Birth of Mondrian, Galería Lirolay, Buenos Aires, Argentina

1971
Off-Center, Salón Auditorio Grimau, Buenos Aires, Argentina
Argentine Painting, Centro Cultural General San Martín, Buenos Aires, Argentina
Emilio Centurión. Tribute to the Master, Galería Arthea, Buenos Aires, Argentina
Boxes and Little Boxes. Centro Cultural General San Martín, Buenos Aires, Argentina

Painting and Geometry, Centro Cultural General San Martín, Buenos Aires, Argentina
LX National Plastic Arts Show, Museo de Arte Decorativo, Buenos Aires, Argentina
Third Italo Show. Energy in Visual Arts, Museo Municipal de Arte Moderno, Buenos Aires, Argentina
Aurora Design Participants, CAyC, Buenos Aires, Argentina
XLII Rosario Show, Museo Municipal de Bellas Artes Juan Castagnino, Rosario, Santa Fe, Argentina
Manuel Belgrano Municipal Plastic Arts Show, Museo Eduardo Sívori, Buenos Aires, Argentina

1970
XVIII Córdoba Plastic Art Show, Museo Provincial de Bellas Artes, Córdoba, Spain
International Painting Festival, Cagnes-sur-Mer, France
Constructive Club, Galería Ales, Prague, Czech Republic
Six Argentine Painters. Art to See and to Have II, Fundación Bariloche, Bariloche, France
24 Argentine Artists, Museo Nacional de Bellas Artes, Buenos Aires, Argentina

1969
Imaginary Show, Gran Hotel Provincial, Mar del Plata, Buenos Aires, Argentina
A Little of Everyone, Galería Lirolay, Buenos Aires, Argentina
Art of Anticipation, Galería Arthea and Revista 2001, Buenos Aires, Argentina
Brizzi, Espinosa, Mac Entyre, Vidal, Biblioteca Popular Esteban Echeverría, Avellaneda, Buenos Aires, Argentina
Exhibition 1969, Patronato del Enfermo de Lepra, Buenos Aires, Argentina
Art to See and to Have, Fundación Bariloche, San Carlos de Bariloche, Rio Negro, Argentina
6 Geometric Painters, Integra Centro de Arte, Buenos Aires, Argentina
Annual Argentine Automobile Club Show. Painting 1969, Automóvil Club Argentino, Buenos Aires, Argentina
The State of Argentine Painting 3. Fundación Lorenzutti, Salas Nacionales de Exposición, Buenos Aires, Argentina

1968–1969
V Tour. Award-Winning Works from the LVI National Show, Argentina

1968
New Ensemble, Museo Nacional de Bellas Artes, Buenos Aires, Argentina
Latest Entries, Museo de Arte Moderno, Buenos Aires, Argentina
Paintings, Sociedad Argentina de Artistas Plásticos, Buenos Aires, Argentina
4 Geometric Painters. Espinosa, Polesello, Silva, Torroja, Galería Arte Nuevo, Buenos Aires, Argentina
LVII National Plastic Arts Show, Salas Nacionales de Exposición, Buenos Aires, Argentina
4 Geometric Painters, Galería Mar del Plata, Mar del Plata, Buenos Aires, Argentina
Materials, New Techniques, New Expressions, Museo Nacional de Bellas Artes, Buenos Aires, Argentina
The 1960s, Sociedad Hebraica Argentina, Buenos Aires, Argentina
Fundación Lorenzutti Prize, Salas Nacionales de Exposición, Buenos Aires, Argentina
Argentine Artists. Works from Paris and Buenos Aires for Rent and for Sale, Instituto Torcuato Di Tella, Buenos Aires, Argentina
Casa Argentina en Israel – Tierra Santa/Primera Plana Plastic Arts Prize, Museo de Arte Moderno, Buenos Aires, Argentina
The Tree of Games, Galería El Taller, Buenos Aires, Argentina

1967–1968
Art in the Air, Museo de Arte Moderno, Buenos Aires, Argentina

1967
First Hisisa Show Dedicated to the Textile Industry, Galería Witcomb, Buenos Aires, Argentina
Different Trends of Current Argentine Painting, Galería de las Artes, Buenos Aires, Argentina
Beyond Geometry. Spread of the Visual Arts Language Today, Centro de Artes Visuales del Instituto Torcuato Di Tella, Buenos Aires, Argentina

Comparisons 67 Show, Musée d'Art Moderne de la Ville de Paris, Paris, France
XXVI Mar del Plata Art Show, Mar del Plata, Buenos Aires, Argentina
LVI National Plastic Arts Show, Salas Nacionales de Exposición, Martín Basa Galería de Arte, Buenos Aires, Argentina

1966
G 13 Group, Roland Lambert Gallery, Buenos Aires, Argentina
Eleven Constructive Painters, Forum Galería de Arte, Buenos Aires, Argentina
First Air France Show, Galería Lascaux, Buenos Aires, Argentina

1965
First Exhibition of Resident Artists in Italy, Casa Argentina, Argentine Embassy, Rome, Italy
Thirteen Resident Painters in Rome, Libreria Feltrinelli, Rome, Italy

1964
Surrealism Imagination, Galería Serra, Buenos Aires, Argentina

1963
Eight Constructive Artists, Museo Nacional de Bellas Artes, Buenos Aires, Argentina
From Concrete Art to the New Tendency. Argentina 1944-1963, Museo de Arte Moderno, Buenos Aires, Argentina

1962
Form and Space, Museo de Arte Contemporáneo, Santiago, Chile

1961
Paintings, Honorable Concejo Deliberante, Buenos Aires, Argentina

1960
Exhibition of Non-Figurative Art, Workshop of Raúl Lozza, Buenos Aires, Argentina

1948
New Realities. Abstract-Concrete-Non-Figurative Art, Galería Van Riel, Buenos Aires, Argentina

1947
Manuel O. Espinosa – Tomás Maldonado, Sociedad Argentina de Artistas Plásticos, Buenos Aires, Argentina

Arte Nuevo, Salón Kraft, Buenos Aires, Argentina
Exhibition of Arte Nuevo, Galería Payes, Buenos Aires, Argentina

1946
First Exhibition of the Asociación Arte Concreto-Invención, Salón Peuser, Buenos Aires, Argentina
Third Exhibition of the Asociación Arte Concreto – Invención, Centro de Profesores Diplomados de Enseñanza Secundaria, Buenos Aires, Argentina
Exhibition of Arte Concreto – Invención, Sociedad Argentina de Artistas Plásticos, Buenos Aires, Argentina
Fourth Exhibition of the Asociación Arte Concreto-Invención, Ateneo Popular de la Boca, Buenos Aires, Argentina

1945
Independent Show (adherent), Galería de Arte Comte, Buenos Aires, Argentina
First Pictorial Exhibition, Círculo Médico del Oeste, Buenos Aires, Argentina

1943
Modern Painting and Tribute to the Vanished Painters, Banco Municipal, Buenos Aires, Argentina
Castagnino, Russo, López Caro, Espinosa, Galería Impulso, Buenos Aires, Argentina

1941–1942
The Martyrdom of Joan of Arc and María the Boatwoman, Cine Arte screening room, Buenos Aires, Argentina

1932
XIII Sign Exhibition. Third CEENA Show, Hotel Castelar, Buenos Aires, Argentina

Awards and Honors (selected)

2001
Castagnino Prize, Museo Municipal de Bellas Artes Juan B. Castagnino, Rosario Artists Stamps, postal stamps from the Fundación Andreani and Fundación arteBA, 2001

1993
Artistic Trajectory, Fondo Nacional de las Artes

1982
Diploma of Merit, Konex Visual Arts Prize

1971
Rotary Club Prize, XVIII Córdoba National Show
Acquisition Grand Prize, Manuel Belgrano Municipal Plastic Arts Show

1969
Argentine Automobile Club Prize

1967
Painting Category Mention Prize, LVI National Plastic Arts Show
Acquisition Prize, Mar del Plata Art Show
First Prize, D category, and Special Mention, A and B categories, First Hisisa Art Show Dedicated to the Textile Industry

1966
Air France Prize, First Air France Painting Show

Public Collections

Fondo Nacional de los Artes, Buenos Aires, Argentina
Jack S. Blanton Museum of Art, Austin, Texas, USA
Museo de Arte Moderno, Buenos Aires, Argentina
Museo Nacional de Bellas Artes, Buenos Aires, Argentina
Museo de Arte Contemporáneo de Caracas Sofía Imber, Caracas, Venezuela
Museum of Art at the Rhode Island School of Design, Providence, Rhode Island, USA
Patricia Phelps de Cisneros Collection, New York, USA

Published in association with the
Sicardi Gallery, Houston on the occasion
of the exhibition *Emanuel Espinosa*
5 February – 8 March 2014
at Stephen Friedman Gallery

Stephen Friedman Gallery
11 & 25–28 Old Burlington Street
London W1S 3AN
www.stephenfriedman.com

Sicardi Gallery
1506 W Alabama Street
Houston, Texas 77006
www.sicardigallery.com

Essay © Cristina Rossi, 2014

Catalogue design: Peter Willberg
Printed in England by PureprintGroup

Photo credits:
Artwork © The Estate of Manuel Espinosa.
Photography by Stephen White, London, Todd
White, London, Oscar Balducci (pages 9 and 12)
and Ariel Gutraich (page 15 and 56).

Cover: Manuel Espinosa, *Untitled*, *c*.1970,
oil on canvas, 150 × 100 cm (59 × 39½ in)

Frontispiece: View of the gallery in the National
Museum of Fine Arts, Buenos Aires (1968).
Photography by Facio Damico.

ISBN 978-0-9575674-9-8

With thanks to Ana Espinosa and the Estate
of Manuel Espinosa.

STEPHEN FRIEDMAN GALLERY

SICARDI GALLERY